If Everybody Did

A Guide to Daily Behavior for Children

JAMEKA WATKINS

INTRODUCTION

One of the most intriguing quotes that I have been acquiring during my youth is "The first rule is no rule!" Sounds so nonsense, right? Why we call a rule "The first rule" whilst there is no rule inside of it? I have been also asking myself that question for a very long time ever since I first heard of it from a movie scene, a martial master imparting earthly moralities to his pupils. That is an interesting point! The true definition of the "vain" rule that I had to spend nearly a decade to be enlightened is breaking old-fashioned rules within establishing a set of new ones ourselves to blueprint as well as take actions toward our ambitions or "one for all" purposes. This very quote plays a core role which has created great humans' huge differences and good values that they have devoted to the civilization of mankind. For instance, we have Bruce Lee, the big martial fighting movies star, the founder of his fighting sect, "Jeet Kune Do". Thought in the starting time of his career when he has just opened his first "Chun Fan Kung Fu" institute in Seattle, America, he had been building up the system of his sect mostly from his teenage background experience of training "Wing Chun Kung Fu" with his former master, Ip Man at Hong Kong. Nevertheless, when he had recognized redundant showy shortcomings in movements, ways of releasing fists, kicks, he decided to "reform" everything by wiping perfunctory movements, vague concepts out and retain useful and real-fighting ones. He has not only broken the stereotypical rule of reformatting a branch of martial art by another but he has also broken one of the most forbidden rules of the Chinese Association in America then. That is propagandizing Kung Fu to Westerns, especially America. Though he had to confront harassing results from the association as well as time-consuming challenging fights that had been set to force him to close his institute and stop teaching foreigner Chinese Kung Fu. However, by his ability and his persistent effort, he has conquered a right to follow up on his desirous dreams. His life is a subsequence of glories and vivid achievements won by himself by being always conforming to the rule of "No rule". But hold on! So is it true that breaking any rule, even the most "unharmed" ones will bring to their "recorder" victories and triumphs?

Not at all! If that is true, there would have never been a set of rules called "inevitable rules" that have been defined by scientists, philosophers, historians, etc. They are those that are boned so that everybody must follow after them unconditionally. Being defeated or trying to resist them, even fighting against those "unwritten regulations" will only hurt you so bad, both on your physical and psychological health. At that time, "The recorder" would turn to "The rule-breaker." Making adults aware of inevitable rules' potential outcomes is a nerves-breaking task to do, but doing the same thing to kids is so much harder. Thus, by using a simple, friendly and deep manner of reciting stories, this book is going to transfer a through core message "There are some rules that you'd better consider to wisely follow in accordance instead of striding to break them out!"

CONTENTS

Chapter 1:
The rule of "Alive and Death"

(Sick and disasters)

"**B**irth, old age, illness, death", the Buddha is long-lived admonition has become a rule and a truth that can be vetoed. For those who are not a believer of Buddhism, you may understand that quote by "chopping" down it into four segments to clarify. "Birth" means appearance, growing, arising of all beings in the vast space. "Old age" means a "peak" where the growth of physical body or exterior values would gradually lay off and be inactive. They would also begin to be worn out within erosion. "Illness" means mental disorder as well as a physical disorder that any living individual may have to encounter with panic and wondering when their life would be taken away by those diseases. "Death" means the end, the time everything is lost and replaced with a new generation that will repeat the same enduring cycle of blooming and growing. Till this point, as if we all can frankly assert that the prayer is not only a temporary rule but a very "eternal truth" because of its circulative feature which makes each period inside of the cycle related to each other closely. The same to catastrophes, if you think "on another planet" tragedies are punishment, results for those who have created sin or karma in the current incarnation of their previous incarnation, then you are wrong. It does not matter whether God plays a complete role in operating the weather as well as making obstacles in our life. The thing is main reasons that cause those disasters, including air pollution, extreme rainfall and flood, earthquake, tsunami, etc. are originated from negative activities of a group or even a majority of unconscious people. As a result, they will have no more choice except for facing the rule of "birth, old age, illness, death". The more they strive to defeat or prevent that rule from hurting them, the more painful they will get by the rule is drastic attack. In the end, whether we could find out some solution to minimize the dreadful affection of this deadly rule? The below useful information mentioned in this chapter would partly give you the answer.

To unlock the question "Whether human beings could refrain nature rules and change their destiny". First of all, we need to redefine the concept of "Destiny".

1. What is destiny?

Destiny is what keeps everything moving forward. Destiny is what generates the motivation to create, to establish, to explore and to fulfill. There is a destiny for you, and there is a destiny for the world. Your destiny here is to find your purpose and to find your allies. The world is destiny is to emerge into the Greater Community. This is where it is heading. It is going in this direction no matter what human society is doing. It must go in this direction. This represents the next stage of your life in the world. It is inevitable and unalterable. That is why we speak of it in terms of destiny instead of in terms of human will and human determination. The need for Knowledge will grow dramatically. There are so many people in the world that have so little, and there are so few that have so much. The resources of the world are shrinking, and the problems of the world are growing. This is seemingly a terrible situation when you put it all together, but it is just the kind of situation that will call people into action—not just an individual here and there who is inspired, but greater numbers of people. The world will be calling them out of their self-preoccupation. The world will be calling them out of their personal interests and tragedies. The world will be demanding things of them. This is what calls your purpose out of you.

2. *Can we change our destiny?*

During the voyage of seeking your purpose, challenge and barricade will probably occur so as to drag you down. So the question is what could you do to "divert" your track to overcome those barriers?

- *You do not have to accept your Destiny:*

With a few extremely rare exceptions, no human being has ever been born into this world without some faults for which they have to make reparation or have some debts to pay. Destiny cannot be moved to pity, but it is never cruel; it is simply just. All the faults you have committed are piled up on one side of the scales, but if you decide to amend your life the good things you do will add weight to the other side of the scales. In this way, when the time comes, your good thoughts, sentiments and actions will be taken into account and your debt will be lighter. This means also that you must not become fatalistic and say, since my destiny is thus and so, there is nothing I can do about it. I just have to accept it.' No; there is one thing you must never forget, and it is this: destiny never wants to stifle or extinguish the spirit. On the contrary, its role is to oblige us to awaken the spirit, to work with the spirit in order to create a new destiny for ourselves.

- *Escape the world of Destiny and enter the world of Providence or Grace:*

Because of the faults committed in previous incarnations, human beings are now subject to destiny. The Hindus say that they have to pay their karma. But this does not mean that there is nothing they can do about it; if they simply lie down under it they will end by being totally crushed. On the contrary, they must fight with weapons of love and light so as to triumph over their destiny and come under the law of providence.

- *Providence is always there, it is a choice:*

Most people have very vague ideas on the subject; they often think that everything that happens to them in life, good or bad, is destiny. No, the words 'destiny' or 'fate' should be used to refer to what happens as a result of your ignorance or your faults, whereas what happens to you as a result of your light and all the good things you have done is providence. So, now this is clear: providence is always there for those who dwell in the light and in divine love, and destiny or fate is the lot of those who persist in their blindness and thoughtlessness.

3. *How to find your mission:*

Firstly, let is distinguish between "Fate" and "Mission". The mission is simply what you are assigned or self-assigned to complete, to a pursuit in your life, and fate is what you do accept as an unhappy fact when you fail your mission. You can change your mission but never give up fate! Though "fate" and "destiny" have the same meaning, the word "fate" is used more negatively to disappoint you and deter you. Only when you have a mission to embark on completing, you can eliminate the risk of thinking about your failures as your fate. So, how to seek and realize our mission? Step by step, I would give you instructions for each stage to proceed.

- *Begin with the right question:*

Don't ask yourself, "What do I want to do with my life?" That is, don't focus on a career. That would be strategy, not a mission. Instead, ask yourself, "What kind of value feels like the most important value I could create?"

- *You're after meaningfulness not passion:*

Thought the two are by no means mutually exclusive, they are distinct from each other. Passion is usually more associated with the strategies you use to fulfill your mission (with sculpting, for example, rather than with a mission to fill the world with beauty).

- *Create a list of 50 things that have brought you great joy in the past and 50 ongoing activities that continue to bring you great joy in the present:*

The point in aiming for 100 items isn't to reach 100 per se but to create an exhaustive list. Including your current job is a good idea; including the aspects of your current job that you enjoy the most is even better.

- *From this list, identify the items that felt the most meaningful to you:*

This is best done by gut feeling. Each item you select should, by definition, be something that in some broad way contributes to the well-being of others.

- *Group these items into related categories:*

Maybe a number of items relate to helping others in a particular way (e.g., with their health, with their talents, or with their relationships). Or maybe to helping people in certain situations (e.g., people living in poverty, who are victims of abuse, or who suffer from mental illness).

- *From these categories, cull out a first draft of a mission statement:*

Two things to keep in mind: This must be a statement derived from experiences you've already had, not ones you'd like to have. You're looking to discover your mission, not invent it (that is, to find what is already there, what already feels like the most important thing you could do with your life, not what you think it is or want it to be). Second, one reasonable litmus test to apply to a candidate statement would entail imagining being presented a lifetime achievement award in your 80s or 90s by the president for having spent your entire life accomplishing it. Does the statement you've come up with hit the sweet spot? That is, when you gut check it, does it feel like the most meaningful thing you could have done?

Only when you have a mission to embark on completing, you can eliminate the risk of thinking about your failures as your fate.

Chapter 2:
The rule of "Limit"
(Patience)

When mentioning the virtue of patience, we can easily exemplify it by a variety of proverbs in Vietnamese folklores that aim to ask descendants for conforming to, such as "Where there is a will, there is a way", "A soft answer turns away wrath", "Practice makes perfect". The word "Patience" is always valuing. Those people who possess that virtue tends to be always trusted to use by higher hierarchies as well as higher social status people. Also, they don't have a habit of chasing immediate advantages but they calmly and minutely make effort to wait for their right moment to the proceeding and achieve longer termed stable ambition. They continually adapt cross-cultural quintessence of the human civilization by readily listening to both praise and criticism to take specific actions day by day and improve themselves and to reach the best version of them. Paradoxically, there is still a minor of community who is also willing to "kneel" under their superiors but they do it in a very such obsequious, even feeble way, or an individual who tends to be hasty and throw himself on a "half-baked-prey" without thinking thoroughly, spending time to think of that action is implicated results if he fails is also considered to be lack of patience. The reason why that minor community exists is simply that their range of patient limit is very finite. It follows that those patient persons are also not impossible to lose their temper. Their range is just further than hot-tempered ones. Still, they also have a "warning point." The rule of the "limit of patience" has been also formed ever since that time. Shall the "Patience" that our ancestors are always teaching us to bear in our mind be "cracked" by exterior and interior factors? Whether people would choose to wait for their "right moment" or suffer by depending on their current circumstances? All of those queries will be "unlocked" in this chapter.

1. Definition of "Patience":

As Maulana Wahiduddin Khan has once said, "Patience is the exercise of restraint in trying situations. It is a virtue, which enables the individual to proceed towards worthy goals which are un-reflected by adverse circumstances or repeated provocations. If he allows himself to become upset by opposition, taunts or other kinds of unpleasantness, he will never reach his goals. He will simply become enmeshed in irrelevancies." When you allow yourself to upset and feel withdraw in your troubles, you have a couple of options to select. One, you would stay calm to analyze your problem, figure out remedies and choose the best one to tackle your problems. The other is to let yourself "sink" into the pessimistic emotion called "suffering."

2. *What is "Suffering"?*

Suffering is usually described as a negative basic feeling or emotion that involves a subjective character of unpleasantness, aversion, harm, or threat of harm. Suffering may be said to be physical or mental, depending whether it refers to a feeling or emotion that is linked primarily to the body or to the mind. Examples of physical suffering are pain, illness, disability, hunger, poverty, and death. Examples of mental suffering are grief, hatred, frustration, heartbreak, guilt, humiliation, anxiety, loneliness, and self-pity. Attitudes towards suffering may vary hugely according to how much one deems it to be light or severe, avoidable or unavoidable, useful or useless, of little or of great consequence, deserved or undeserved, chosen or unwanted, acceptable or unacceptable. Physical suffering can often be ameliorated by medical, political, and economic measures that can alleviate disease and poverty and put an end to conflicts and wars. Mental suffering persists, however, even in the most ideal physical circumstances. Even as regards to physical suffering, science offers no cure for the ultimate physical suffering-death. Suffering is endemic to the human condition, and the ways people address suffering go far in determining the course of their lives. People can be defeated and embittered by suffering, or they can use their suffering to spur them on to a successful life. Awareness of the suffering of others can motivate charity and a life of public service. Some people even take suffering on themselves in order to relieve the suffering of others. Suffering can also lead to realizations about the purpose of life and open a door to transcendence.

3. *Outcomes of depression:*

If you have few experiences in suffering from "nerves-breaking" time, you've already how hard it was to sustain "depression". Your mental wounds are always the first reason causes it. Most of us tend to look down on its potential outcomes and that unawareness leads us to the brink of getting more dangerous diseases, such as autism, hypotension, even stroke. Depression can cause a lot of symptoms within the central nervous system, many of which are easy to dismiss or ignore.

Older adults may also have difficulty identifying cognitive changes because it is easy to dismiss the signs of depression as related to "getting older." According to the American Psychological Association, older adults with depression have more difficulties with memory loss and reaction time during everyday activities compared with younger adults with depression. Symptoms of depression include overwhelming sadness, grief, and a sense of guilt. It may be described as a feeling of emptiness or hopelessness. Some people may find it difficult to put these feelings into words. It may also be difficult for them to understand as symptoms can manifest and cause physical reactions. Frequent episodes of crying may be a symptom of depression, although not everyone who is depressed cries. You may also feel tired all the time or have trouble sleeping at night. Other symptoms include: irritability, anger, and loss of interest in things that used to bring pleasure, including sex. Depression can cause headaches, chronic body aches, and pain that may not respond to medication. It is also sometimes an effect of certain neurological diseases, such as Alzheimer is disease, epilepsy, and multiple sclerosis. People with depression may have trouble maintaining a normal work schedule or fulfilling social obligations. This could be due to symptoms such as an inability to concentrate, memory problems, and difficulty making decisions. Some people who are depressed may turn to alcohol or drugs, which may increase instances of reckless or abusive behavior. Someone with depression may consciously avoid talking about it or try to mask the problem. People experiencing depression may also find themselves preoccupied with thoughts of death or hurting themselves. While there is a 25 times greater risk of suicide, even during the recovery process, the American Association of Suicidology reports that treatment for depression is effective 60 to 80 percent of time.

While depression is often thought of as a mental illness, it also plays a heavy role in appetite and nutrition. Some people cope by overeating or bingeing. This can lead to weight gain and obesity-related illnesses, such as type 2 diabetes. You may even lose your appetite entirely, or fail to eat the right amount of nutritious food. A sudden loss of interest in eating in older adults can lead to a condition called geriatric anorexia. It is important to maintain a healthy diet when experiencing depression. Nutrients are essential to making sure the body is neurotransmitters are firing right.

Depression and stress are closely related. Stress hormones speed heart rate and make blood vessels tighten, putting your body in a prolonged state of emergency. Over time, this can lead to heart disease. Untreated, depression raises the risk of dying after a heart attack. Heart disease is also a trigger for depression. The Cleveland Clinic estimates that about 15 percent of people with heart disease also develop major depression. Depression and stress may have a negative impact on the immune system, making you more vulnerable to infections and diseases. One review looked at studies and found that there seemed to be a relationship between inflammation and depression, although the exact connection is unclear. Inflammation is linked to many illnesses, such as stress. Some anti-inflammatory agents have shown to benefit some people with depression.

4. Tips to be more patient and exclude yourself from depression:

- *Make Yourself Wait:*

The best way to practice patience is to make yourself wait. A study published in Psychological Science shows that waiting for things actually makes us happier in the long run. Start with something small like waiting a few extra minutes to drink that milkshake and then move on to something bigger. You will begin to gain more patience as you practice.

- *Stop Doing Things That Aren't Important:*

We all have things in our lives that take time away from what is important. One way of removing stress from our lives is to stop doing those things. Take a few minutes and evaluate your week. Look at your schedule from when you wake up to the time you go to sleep. Take out two or three things that you do that aren't important but take time. It is time to learn to say no to things that cause stress and make us impatient.

- *Be Mindful of the Things Making You Impatient:*

Most people have several tasks in their head, and they jump from thought to thought without taking the time to finish one task first. We live interrupted lives as we try to multitask and it is frustrating when we feel we aren't making progress. It is better to be mindful of our thoughts and the best way to understand this is to write down what makes you impatient. This will help you slow down and focus on one task at a time and remove those things that stress you out.

- *Relax and Take Deep Breaths:*

Most of all, just relax and take deep breaths. Taking slow deep breaths can help calm the mind and body. This is the easiest way to help ease any impatient feelings you are experiencing. If breathing doesn't help I find taking a walk to clear your head can be helpful in getting refocused on what is important. The point is to find some time for you each day to decompress.

- *Understand & Counteract Your Triggers:*

Impatience is something that is triggered. This trigger is different for everybody but it has the same purpose. To become more patient try to "understand" what your trigger is. What is that thing that you think about or feel right before you lose it? Maybe your trigger is when someone screams at you? or if someone calls you a certain name? Point is whatever your trigger, the first step to countering it is to understand it and try to uncover the deep-rooted insecurity that is causing this trigger to exist in the first place.

Once you understand what your trigger is you can work on counteracting it by doing calming exercises or techniques whenever you feel the trigger building up.

- *Increase Your Self-Confidence:*

Impatience usually rears its ugly head when you feel let down or when you don't feel in control or perhaps feel that your hands are tied. You want something to happen now, but you just cannot seem to do anything to speed things up. A person with a high level of confidence will accept the situation as it is; they will not fight it or rail against it. Rather, they will work with it. To become more patient, realize that patience and confidence go hand in hand. A good example I like using is of rafting in the ocean. If you try to paddle against the tide you will exert a lot of energy and will feel extremely tired, yet against the power of waves, won't travel that far of a distance. But if you paddle with the current, not just will you exert very little energy, you will also travel a much further distance. In life, you have to pick and choose your battles. Sure there are times you must take a stand and travel against the current, but in most day to day moments, it is not just healthier but also much easier to go with the flow of things and have the confidence to deal with life as it happens.

- *Put On Your "Positive" Glasses:*

For example, if you miss your bus don`t focus on the negatives but emphasize the positive things such as you`ll get exercise from walking or that you can enjoy the fresh air. So try to put a positive spin on everything you do; you will find that you will not just reduce tension but you`ll become a much happier person. Michael Jordan once said, "Always turn a negative situation into a positive situation."

- *Change Your Attitude:*

Most people struggling with patience can never answer this question.

"Why are you in such a hurry?" Realize that even if something happens a few seconds or even a few minutes late, nothing will happen (If your job requires you or your team members to be extremely punctual, that is a different topic altogether. The scope of this article is more about being patient in day to day life) The task will still get done and everything will still work out. Try to keep an open perspective and don't give yourself useless stress.

- *Visualize Worst-Case Scenarios :*

This might seem counterproductive, but if you try to be one step ahead of the game by visualizing yourself facing the problem before it happens. This lets you set goals for how you are going to react and react in a more positive way when faced with that stressing situation. A lack of patience is really just insecurity packaged differently. You are impatient and not able to "handle the pressure" and succumb to letting go because you are not ready to deal with the consequences of not getting what you want right away. For example, after a long hard day if you have requested your spouse or child to bring you some water, but they are late and don't bring it right away, and you lose your cool — is this a problem in them or a problem in you? Why can't you wait for longer? What is the worst-case scenario? Is simply some temporary dryness of your throat the only real "negative" to you waiting? You should ask yourself similar questions like these in every situation when you feel your patience running thin. You will discover there are very few real-life scenarios your body is not fit to withstand or tolerate.

- *Periodically Release Tension and Stress:*

In most cases, impatience is the release of pent up stress, tension, and anxiety. Say you had a long day at work, and your boss was grilling you all day long. But because if you talk back to your boss you can get fired, you "tolerate it" and absorb all of that negative energy and stress. But unfortunately just like physics, once any object absorbs energy or better said it is energy level increases (for example a rock lifted off the ground, now has the innate energy inside of it to fall down due to gravity), the energy is never destroyed but only converted. So sometimes people who seem impatient aren't really to blame at all, they just are not able to release this pent up energy inside of them correctly and instead leaks out during moments of stress.

"Patience is power, not an absence of action."

Chapter 3:
The rule of the finiteness of everything

In a Vietnamese folklore, there is an adage considered "Forest is gold, the ocean is silver, oceans of money" which refers to the diverse wealth of natural resources as well as minerals of a certain region or a country. Vietnam and its worldwide second highest quantity of coffee or African nations with its vast nuggets of cruel oil and precious metals could exemplify that adage. That is the reason why they used to be very intriguing prey in the eyes of imperial countries, such as the US, Russia, Portugal, etc. But when the reunification has been back, whilst nations' economy was gradually recovering and galloping, a very sad paradox has arisen. While Korea and Japan where are essentially lack of resources and population-stressed have made a leaped to become two of top-economic countries in the world, those two which I mentioned at the beginning where fundamentally possess an "extravagant wardrobe" of natural resources, as well as endless workforces, have been facing resources-scarcity; extinction of a host of endangered species; indebtedness annually increases; serious environmental pollution. The question that I would like to ask you for seeking it answers that whether the adage "Forest is gold, the ocean is silver" is completely right nowadays or not? Could you denote the relation between the rule of "the finiteness of everything" and that quote? What are the causes of that rule and could we be capable of doing something to prevent outcomes if we fail in maintaining it?

1. Do everything last forever?

In the grand scheme of things, you don't matter at all. Yet, at the very same time, you need to exist in order for the universe to exist in the state that it is existing -- so in a sense, you are indispensable. This is the paradox that we're all part of. We both matter and don't matter. We both can change the future, yet can't leave a deep enough mark for the universe to even notice.

Sooner or later, if the Big Bang Theory is spot-on, the universe and time itself will come to an end. Knowing this, it is easy to understand one is true insignificance. No matter what you do, what you change, what you believe, it will all be over someday. Of course, chances are that the human race will have been long extinct by then, but nevertheless, it is a fascinating truth. The only thing that lasts is destruction, which is most likely why human beings are so keen on killing and destroying -- it is the one thing that is eternal. Other than that, nothing lasts forever. Nothing at all. However, whether this is good news or bad news is really up for interpretation. The bad news: Nothing lasts forever. The good news: Nothing lasts forever. The only things in the universe that matter are the things that matter to people and other living things with some level of consciousness.

Nothing lasts forever, so your decisions won't, either. This should give you some solace; no matter how much you screw up, your mistakes and any repercussions they incur won't last the test of time. Sure, people may still suffer as a result, but even their suffering will inevitably come to an end. Everything you dedicated your life to, everything you did, created, built and found to be of significant importance will one day disappear. Nothing in the universe, including the universe, lasts forever. If you're smart, you will use the little time that you have to make the most of it. If you want your life to matter then you have to decide that it does; no one else will ever decide that for you.

2. *The relation between the rule of the finiteness of everything and the biodiversity loss:*

Like I was stating above, occurrence of the rule will implicate many related consequences. One of typical examples for them is the loss of the biodiversity. Exploiting nuggets, resources or hunting wild animals overwhelmingly will lead the balance of biodiversity to the brink of being "shattered."

Biodiversity is critical for maintaining ecosystem health. Declining biodiversity lowers an ecosystem is productivity (the amount of food energy that is converted into the biomass) and lowers the quality of the ecosystem is services (which often include maintaining the soil, purifying water that runs through it, and supplying food and shade, etc.). Biodiversity loss also threatens the structure and proper functioning of the ecosystem. Although all ecosystems are able to adapt to the stresses associated with reductions in biodiversity to some degree, biodiversity loss reduces an ecosystem is complexity, as roles once played by multiple interacting species or multiple interacting individuals are played by fewer or none. Reduced biodiversity also creates a kind of "ecosystem homogenization" across regions as well as throughout the biosphere. Specialist species (i.e., those adapted to narrow habitats, limited food resources, or other specific environmental conditions) are often the most vulnerable to dramatic population declines and extinction when conditions change. On the other hand, generalist species (those adapted to a wide variety of habitats, food resources, and environmental conditions) and species favored by human beings (i.e., livestock, pets, crops, and ornamental plants) become the major players in ecosystems vacated by specialist species. As specialist species and unique species (as well as their interactions with other species) are lost across a broad area, each of the ecosystems in the area loses some amount of complexity and distinctiveness, as the structure of their food chains and nutrient-cycling processes become increasingly similar. Biodiversity loss affects economic systems and human society. Humans rely on various plants, animals, and other organisms for food, building materials, and medicines, and their availability as commodities is important to many cultures. The loss of biodiversity among these critical natural resources threatens global food security and the development of new pharmaceuticals to deal with future diseases. Simplified, homogenized ecosystems can also represent an aesthetic loss.

3. *How to exclude from being lost biodiversity and abstain from overusing consume goods?*

Governments, nongovernmental organizations, and the scientific community must work together to create incentives to conserve natural habitats and protect the species within them from unnecessary harvesting, while deterring behavior that contributes to habitat loss and degradation. Sustainable development (economic planning that seeks to foster growth while preserving environmental quality) must be considered when creating new farmland and human living spaces. Laws that prevent poaching and the indiscriminate trade in wildlife must be improved and enforced. . Efforts that monitor the status of individual species, such as the Red List of Threatened Species from the International Union for Conservation of Nature and Natural Resources (IUCN) and the United States Endangered Species list remain critical tools that help decision makers prioritize conservation efforts. In addition, a number of areas rich in unique species that could serve as priorities for habitat protection have been identified.

Cutting down on wasting your family budget also plays such significant role in balancing the biodiversity because of staying away from consuming wild-animals originated goods. Here are the list of twelve mini tips which you can easily do to save your life.

- *Set savings goals:*

It is always good to make a plan. Are you saving your money in order to buy a car? Perhaps you just want to pay down those credit card balances. Whatever the case, set your goals. Once you have a clear idea of what you are saving for, you will be prepared to work toward that goal. Think of your goals as a line of defense protecting you from spending inordinately.

- *Plan your budget:*

Keep track of what you are spending, and log daily entries into a budget spreadsheet. Over time, you will see how much you spend every day, week, month, and year. If you need some help, there are many effective budget planners that you can find using a search engine. You can analyze your budget, and pinpoint exactly where your wallet is hemorrhaging. You can also keep track of your income in the same manner – make sure that you are not spending more than you earn! In any case, simply cut out the expenses that aren't doing anything for your savings, and watch your earnings grow.

- *Balance before you spend:*

Pay all of your bills before you leave the house to go out. When you are unaware of your financial condition, you are more likely to spend money frivolously. When you have a good idea of your finances, however, your awareness will help you when you go out. Balancing your checkbook will provide you with the willpower to avoid spending too much.

- *Wait three days:*

Whenever you are tempted to make a big purchase, wait three days. While you're waiting, consider whether or not you need what you want to buy. After the rush of impulse shopping wears off, you will know if it is something you actually want to purchase.

- *Eat your food:*

Don't go out to eat. There is food in your fridge that is probably better for you, and you will save big bucks by staying home. Check your pantry before you take another trip to the store: you probably have some food in there too. And when you do go to the store, eat before you go – a hungry shopper is a "wasting" one! Remember, only go to the store when the food is gone. You will take fewer trips and lower your grocery bill, effectively saving you some money in the process.

- *Pack your lunch:*

Many people spend their money daily on expensive restaurants and food trucks. Avoid this trap by making a sack lunch before you leave the house for work. You will eat healthier, and you will save a great deal of money by following this tip.

- *Buy good quality and use it:*

It is common for people to almost never use the things they love the most, a favorite pair of jeans, a vintage Mustang and that give them the most pleasure. Why? Often, it is because they want to protect the item in question, because they like it so much and don't want it to be ruined. Instead of using their favorites regularly, they buy cheaper things, sometimes knockoff imitations for "everyday" use. The unfortunate result is less satisfaction, and that lack of satisfaction often leads to more buying in the misguided hope that some new item will make us happier. In a similar vein, many people spend more money on an outfit they wear once for a special occasion than they spend the entire year on clothing they use every week, such as workout wear, jeans, or sneakers. The smarter approach is to put your money where you will see it in action and enjoy it the most, thereby reducing purchasing cravings.

- *Count your blessings:*

First and foremost, being grateful, not just for possessions, but also for the people, places and simple pleasures in life is good for the soul. But an attitude of gratitude is also a proven antidote to impulse purchasing because it creates a sense of abundance within the individual. When you're feeling full of gratitude, you're less likely to subconsciously try to fill emotional holes by treating yourself with gifts and accumulating more stuff.

- *Focus on the bottom line, not freebies:*

"Free" is the four-letter word that always seems to work in marketing. But the free gift with purchase, the free bottle of water while you're shopping and the free samples can all cost your wallet. For one thing, getting something for free creates a sense of obligation that makes it harder to say "no" to a persuasive salesperson. Shoppers also often use the free gifts included with purchase to rationalize buying something that is way beyond their budget.

- *Remember that it is okay to buy nothing:*

Shopping takes time, and it can feel like time wasted if a purchase isn't made. Outlet malls, which typically require a significant drive, are particularly dangerous places for people trying to reduce their consumption. It is not uncommon for people to purchase something they don't really need rather than to leave empty-handed, with the feeling like the trip was a total waste. The same phenomenon occurs in upscale "destination" boutiques and at e-retail sites that have drawn shoppers in for significant amounts of time. But don't fall for the notion that you've wasted time if you shop and don't buy. The truth is that buying something you don't need only makes for more waste.

- *Shop for stuff you need, not sales:*

Another of the psychological reasons that many people over-shop and buy is to get a burst of feel-good dopamine that accompanies sale shopping. Snagging a coveted item at 30% off can feel like winning a prize. But sales are nothing special: Virtually everything is discounted at some point in today is retail world, and at least three-quarters of the purchases shoppers tell me they regret making were bought on sale. They often say they the item isn't quite the right size, color, shape, or style, but what got them hooked was that the price was right. This is silly, of course. If you don't like the item, there is no price that makes it a smart buy.

- *Buy for the right reasons:*

Research shows that we can think we're hungry when we're actually thirsty, think we're tired when in reality we're bored, and so forth. In other words, we're pretty good at identifying when we need something, just not so good at identifying precisely what it is we need. The concept translates directly into the world of shopping and buying: People often buy stuff not because they truly need the stuff, but to fill a variety of other psychological needs, including the craving for human contact, relief from boredom, the opportunity to feel totally competent and in control, and the mental stimulation of something unique or beautiful. To buy less, don't confuse the real reasons you're shopping

"Take action to protect the biodiversity now to protect yourself and maintain the inevitability of the rule of the definiteness of everything."

Chapter 4:
The rule of getting involved
("The crowd" and "The outsider")

The fourth rule that the author would love to refer to in this book is not a complete "inevitable rule" which means you can do nothing to change its consequences, no matter you want it to happen or not. This is because the derivation of "the rule of getting involved" (also called "the rule of herds" in the world of animal beings) is not "molded" by the Mother Nature but artificially created in very mindset, notion, attitude and action of human beings. To break it down to you, the author will borrow a quote from Lu Bu in the best-known series of the novel "Three Kingdoms" written by the famous novelist Luó Guànzhong: "In an age when everybody is naked, one who wears pants is a pervert." Up to now, as if you've understood the author's intention when selecting the title of this chapter. In a society where "the crowd" follow each other to do silly, senseless things, an "outsider" who walk an opposite side of their road would be immediately considered to be a weirdo, a wacko, even be said to be worth being inexistent in their world because he (or she) didn't let himself (herself) get involved into a riot of that crowd. Doing something right which is not in favor of the crowd's conservative rigid wrongdoings is completely different from going against moralities that are priorities of what human beings ought to conform. "An outsider" that the author mentioned is the one who obtains an advanced mindset and he (or she) is in hope of making differences as well as bring good values back to a new society and alter an old-fashioned one. The author doesn't mean to exhort an idea of being apathetic neglectful ones to surroundings. The rule that seems to be a variable one to nobody but it will going to be if there are none of those "outsiders" who recognize wrongness in the crowd's ideology and they are willing to stand in an opposite "fighting-line" to the crowd.

1. Why people follow the crowd?

In a study by French psychologists Serge Moscovici and Marisa Zavalloni, researchers asked participants some questions. First, researchers asked about their opinion of the French president. Second, they asked about their attitude toward Americans. The researchers then asked the participants to discuss each topic as a group. After a discussion, groups who held a tentative consensus became more extreme in their opinions. For example, participants held slightly favorable attitudes toward the French president. But their attitudes magnified as group members spoke with one another. They held slightly negative attitudes toward Americans. But their attitudes intensified as each member learned others shared their views about their allies abroad. The researchers concluded, "Group consensus seems to induce a change of attitudes in which subjects are likely to adopt more extreme positions." When we see our uncertain opinions reflected back to us, our beliefs strengthen. There is a heuristic most of us use to determine what to do, think, say, and buy: the principle of social proof. To learn what is correct, we look at what other people are doing. Social proof is a shortcut to decide how to act.

One reason why do others influence us so much is that we live in a complex world. We use the decisions of others as a heuristic, or mental shortcut, to navigate our lives. Advertisers don't have to persuade us that a product is good, they only need to say others think so. Following the crowd allows us to function in a complicated environment. Most of us do not have time to increase our knowledge of all merchandise and research every advertised item to measure its usefulness. Instead, we rely on signals like popularity. If everyone else is buying something, the reasoning goes, there is a good chance the item is worth our attention. A second reason others influence us is that humans are social. We have survived because of our ability to band together. Early humans who formed groups were more likely to survive. This affected our psychology. In our evolutionary past, our ancestors were under constant threat. Keen awareness of others helped our ancestors survive in a dangerous and uncertain world. Modern humans have inherited such adaptive behaviors. These behaviors include banding together and promoting social harmony. This includes not dissenting from the group. In a hunter-gatherer group, being ostracized or banished could have been a death sentence.

2. *Why we shouldn't follow the crowd?*

A study has been done to figure out the psychology of a person when he is trying to answer a certain question when there is an opinion of a whole group involved. Basically, the results of the study were that scores of people who thought they had an answer to a question were decreased tremendously when the group voiced their answer. The reason behind this is that in the individual person's mind, the more people have the same answer, the more that group has power and influence over the decision of someone else. People let go of their development of the thinking brain and forces people to stop coming up with their own opinions about given situations. This can lead to things like dependence and inability to critically think and come up with your own opinion. The crowd may be completely wrong about something but will be believed by everyone because many people followed and in the end whatever that crowd says will almost in all cases be believed as true. When people form a group they usually infect each other with their incorrect beliefs and together they come to see an even more distorted reality. Unless a person is brave enough not to lie to himself and unless a person has enough courage to be different his presence in a group will only let him see reality from a different angle.

3. How to stop following the crowd a avoid "Herd mentality"?

Today, societal trends overpower talent and hard work, making it difficult to truly shine. Standing out and being yourself is the only way to stay real and not be corrupted by corporate branding and their fabrication of images. Striving to grab attention, we exploit our physical appearance for social media followings and popularity. But reality is not what we see on media platforms, rather it lives in the hearts of the innocent and the "real". "Real" people are those who go against socially constructed laws and do not believe in conformity and they are ready to stand out of the crowd and speak out what they believed that it's true. Don't bury yourself trying follow society because their standards of perfection are out of reach. Don't forget, it's your life, your mindset, your body. No one else is living it; only you are. Imagine you are the front seat driver of your life. Take the wheel and drive in the direction of your will. Strive towards your dreams, regardless of how scary it might seem. And always keep in mind that everyone around you lives with their insecurities and weaknesses, but it does not mean you must follow their beliefs to feel acceptance and peace.

Here is a list of ten tips that can help you prevent your children from going down the wrong path of friendships and following the wrong crowd as well as exclude them from the "Herd mentality".

- *Want:*

Children often want those toys that belong to someone else, very much! Adults do this too! We all have to learn to be happy with what we have, not with what our neighbors have. Teach them to take special care of what they do have and that what they have is very special. Show them that there are others that have much less or nothing at all. We need to learn to be content with what God has provided for us.

- *Lying:*

Making things up, exaggerating and stretching the truth is in any form a lie. Exaggerating seems like a harmless thing, but when you think about it, it is a lie. Some children don't know where the limit is in making up stories or exaggerating. This can easily turn into the habit of lying. When we lie, the natural progression is to follow others that lie too. Gossip and rumors follow in these crowds. If you notice your child exaggerating or spreading rumors, sit them down and explain how these type of lies can hurt people and their own self-image.

- *Stealing:*

When a child wants something so bad, they can easily be swayed into stealing. If they are in a crowd that encourages them, then stealing can become a habit. Children need to learn at an early age that taking another child's toy is not ok. Stealing always hurts someone. If an item is taken, then it must be returned as soon as you notice that your child has stolen it.

- *Cheating:*

This one often happens when children are playing games. They feel in order to get ahead, they need to cheat and be deceitful. However, they don't think they are doing anything wrong. They just want to be the winner. When they are teens and have followed this way of life, they will go along with the crowd to cheat on friends, girlfriends and boyfriends and into the future with committing adultery. Start now by teaching them to play fair, that it's ok to lose and honor those that have won.

- *Killing:*

Seems extreme, right? But if you think about it, how often are your children already killing something? I'm not against video games (completely) but are your children killing in video games? Are they playing these games every day and being programmed that killing is a normal everyday occurrence? Look over the games and apps they are engaging in. If it's a possibility the game is leading them down the wrong path, and associating with the wrong type of friends, you may want to limit play time or ban certain games.

- *Respect:*

First, children need to learn to respect their parents. In order for children to respect their parents, parents need to be worthy of that respect. It's hard to respect a parent that cheats, lies and steals. When children respect their parents, they learn to respect others as well. If your child hangs around other children that are disrespectful to their parents, it's only a matter of time before you child will follow suit. Take your child aside and explain why that type of behavior is not ok. And also tell them the right way to behave and proper things to say to an adult if they don't agree with that adult.

- *Rest:*

Taking a day out of the week to rest from the overwhelming everyday tasks can be vital to a child. We often run and run and run, dragging our children along with us. We must first show our children why it's important to take a restful or Sabbath day. We can better prepare for the week ahead. We can be ready for the attacks against us and be prepared to stand up for what is right. Children need this rest. They are around so many people each day and are experiencing new things at a rate that would make our heads spin. Give them a fighting chance to stay away from the wrong crowd with a rest.

- *Speaking:*

Words are so powerful, more so than most people think. They can lift you up or tear you down. We need to be so careful and gentle with our words, especially when speaking to children. We are bombarded by profanity, insults, verbal abuse, and every day by media, peers and even family. Protect your children as much as possible from these hurtful sources. If our children get accustomed to these words, they will use them and hang around people that use them all the time.

- *Idols:*

Who do your children look up to? Is it the latest pop-star or sports figure? If children learn to look up to the most popular kid in school or big-hit actor on their favorite show, they will easily follow the "popular" kid in the wrong crowd. Sometimes teaching a child to give away some of their toys for another child can help them to learn that items are not of the greatest importance.

- *Trust:*

Trust is a huge matter. Just as children, especially teens are to earn our trust. We must give good reason for our children to trust us. If we use "little-white-lies" or any type of deceit with our children, they will never learn to trust us whole-heartily. When you tell them why it's important to not follow that certain crowd, do you want them to trust you or not?

"*Stop trying to reach others' standards and be happy with your life. Bear in your mind that you are always a unique.*"

Chapter 5:
"Gravitational Theory"

During the time the brilliant physicist Isaac Newton was researching for his "Gravitational Theory", an object which is "m" of weight will tend to gravitate to another which is "M" of weight with an acceleration "g". Respectively, "G" represents the "gravitational constant" and "r" represents the distance between two things. Among those parameters, the "force of gravity" which both affect each other is the same and there are contradictory. An intriguing point that as if most of us have already known is that the formation of the gravitational theory is originated from being hit by an apple on Newton's head while he was taking a nap at noon. Nobody then knew that the very event has "seeded" a big physical theory to change the whole viewpoint of the whole era. Correspondingly, the question which is posed by the author is whether there is a "gravitational force" between us, human beings? Yes, it is! Newton's theory has been acknowledged to be true to all creatures or existing on Earth or objects in the universe. In short, we can assertively conclude that this rule is inevitable. But the real "gravity" that the author would like to emphasize here is not only the natural physical beauty and irresistible of partners in a conversation but also material, psychological or even mental condition of human beings' impact on each other so that produce sequences of limitless links in the community. I have got a very favorite saying, "Everything among the universe is bound by reluctant or voluntary rapports which are unable to be crashed." That quote completely denies explainable old-schooled perspective considers, "Those who don't live their life will be punished by God!" which is always being accepted in Chinese culture as well as Southeast Asian culture. We cannot live a quiet isolated life from the community but we have to continually create "gravitational force" on those people around us. Without more ado, let's dive into this last chapter to come to clean why the truth of this rule.

1. Everything is related:

Like I was saying, everything in the universe has its influencing sphere of gravitational force. By the geographical distance between objects or creatures, they will have various levels of the force of gravity to have an impact on their "target". Thereby assumption considers everything is related is evident.

Creation is the ultimate act of divine revelation. And that revelation requires both the 'natural' world and the products of human culture. Humans are not (just) the audience to whom God is revealed, we are part of the very picture of revelation itself. Humans are necessarily and essentially part of the created realm. Creation is not just the stage on which the human drama plays out. Creation is not just the background, setting, or home that gives a place for humans to live, as if the only thing that really matters, in the grand scheme of things, is human culture. Creation is also not some smooth-running machine into which the monkey wrench of human civilization has unfortunately been thrown. If creation is not just here to serve our purposes, neither are we, as humans, here merely to serve its purposes or to be wished away if we are unwilling to fall in line with creation's goals. To see the whole of our world, we must realize that world is not just about things. It's also about the way those things relate to each other. The world is not just stuff, it is an intricate web, a delicate weave.

Unfortunately, our relationships with other people or other creatures is not as simple as are the relationships of the stadium-goers involved in making the giant picture. We have to acknowledge and respect the different ways of relating, since a 'bad relationship' might actually have some pretty good ways of relating mixed with some other bad ways of relating. Being aware of these different modes of relating therefore proves quite helpful in living our life. Give us a better sense of how to proceed wisely and faithfully in our everyday lives. This, in turn, helps us get a better sense of our relationships with the things around us, both what is good in those relationships and what might not be so good.

2. Why should we care for lower statuses, especially poor?

It will be so nonsense when you think the life of people of other lower statuses doesn't influence yours. They do in so many domains. That is the reason why I told you that we were all related to any kind of things surround us. Let me demonstrate to you why should we care for them.

First, poverty means wasted lives of people who could have grown to their full potential, prospered, and contributed. How many could have become doctors, scientists, professionals, and contributors to the well-being of their families, friends, and society at large? Second, poverty breeds desperation and leads some desperate poor people into wasted lives, in some extremes even to crime. Beggars abound in poor countries; in some cases they are even organized as a business. Some who are deprived of good things turn to criminal activities, such as burglary, holdups, prostitution, or drug running. The victims of crime include the poor themselves as well as many members of society at large. How many could be organized and supported to become productive instead of destructive? Third, the poor are more prone to illnesses and health problems. Consider that in today's fast-moving world, diseases travel at breakneck speeds. Although it took decades for AIDS to spread, the bird flu showed signs of doing that in months. Those with only a few fowl to provide eggs and a few underfed chickens to eat will not destroy their only food source to save someone from the bird flu living in a land they have never seen. Fourth, the poor represent far more than a group that deserves our sympathy and charity. Helping the poor escape from poverty will also help raise the incomes of the rest of the world. The poor constitute a major untapped market opportunity for businesses that can imagine new ways to bring down the cost of products and services to the poor. A fifth reason that more advanced nations should worry about nations filled with poor people. These nations often collapse into "failed states" that fall into conflicts and violence that necessitate military intervention by U.S. or NATO or UN forces. This happened with Honduras, Lebanon, Somalia, and Bosnia-Herzegovina, each violent outbreak within or between countries posing a threat to U.S. and European national security.

To sum up, from now on, we have to get started to be aware of the significant role that each of us is playing for this world and don't forget to get connected to more and more people so that we can make a bind relates us much more unbreakable.

"Each of us is always related to each other. No matter you would like to admit or not. That is the truth."

CONCLUSION

The only hope that the author would like you to bear in your mind is that you should block out at least an hour per day to be experienced in observing what you have done to change an awkward circumstance's results or prevent its dire outcomes. Meanwhile, introspect whether you had forced yourself to break any inevitable rule's "deadly boundary" which is mentioned in the book. After testing yourself, consolidate those lessons you have acquired to put them into forthcoming challenging practical situations. Last but not least, take time before getting on the bed every night to recite what you have done to tackle your issues but concurrently, you have not broken any of those rules which we'd better "flow" with them instead of striving to win them. I wish you would have been leading your child to walk on the right track to honesty and success. Have a nice day.

ABOUT THE AUTHOR

Jameka Watkins is the New York Times bestselling author of The Joy of Leaving Your Sh*t All Over the Place. She is also the author of Cocktails for Drinkers, Poetry from Scratch and the novel Afloat. Her work has appeared in the Atlantic, Teen Vogue and on BBC Radio 4.

www.ingramcontent.com/pod-product-compliance
Lightning Source LLC
Chambersburg PA
CBHW030410160726
47992CB00007B/3051